D0174862

BELIEVE

Hope Has Your Name on It

JOEL OSTEEN

Faith
Words

NASHVILLE • NEW YORK

Also by Joel Osteen

ALL THINGS ARE WORKING
FOR YOUR GOOD
*Daily Readings from All Things Are
Working for Your Good*

BLESSED IN THE DARKNESS
Blessed in the Darkness Journal
Blessed in the Darkness Study Guide

BREAK OUT!
Break Out! Journal
Daily Readings from Break Out!

DIGEST BOOKS
Stay in the Game
The Abundance Mind-set
*Two Words That Will Change Your Life
Today*

EMPTY OUT THE NEGATIVE
A Fresh New Day Journal

EVERY DAY A FRIDAY
Every Day a Friday Journal
Daily Readings from Every Day a Friday

FRESH START
Fresh Start Study Guide

I DECLARE
I Declare Personal Application Guide

NEXT LEVEL THINKING
Next Level Thinking Journal
Next Level Thinking Study Guide
Daily Readings from Next Level Thinking

PEACEFUL ON PURPOSE
Peaceful on Purpose Study Guide
Peace for the Season

PSALMS AND PROVERBS FOR
EVERYDAY LIFE

RULE YOUR DAY
Rule Your Day Journal

THE POWER OF FAVOR
The Power of Favor Study Guide

THE POWER OF I AM
The Power of I Am Journal
The Power of I Am Study Guide
Daily Readings from The Power of I Am

THINK BETTER, LIVE BETTER
Think Better, Live Better Journal
Think Better, Live Better Study Guide
*Daily Readings from Think Better,
Live Better*

WITH VICTORIA OSTEEN
Our Best Life Together
Wake Up to Hope Devotional

YOU ARE STRONGER THAN YOU THINK
*You Are Stronger Than You Think
Study Guide*

YOU CAN, YOU WILL
You Can, You Will Journal
Daily Readings from You Can, You Will

YOUR BEST LIFE NOW
Your Best Life Begins Each Morning
Your Best Life Now for Moms
Your Best Life Now Journal
Your Best Life Now Study Guide
Daily Readings from Your Best Life Now
*Scriptures and Meditations for
Your Best Life Now*
Starting Your Best Life Now

YOUR GREATER IS COMING
Your Greater Is Coming Study Guide

BELIEVE

FaithWords
Hachette Book Group
1290 Avenue of the Americas
New York, NY 10104
faithwords.com
twitter.com/faithwords

First Edition: June 2023

FaithWords is a division of Hachette Book Group, Inc. The FaithWords name and logo are trademarks of Hachette Book Group, Inc.

The publisher is not responsible for websites (or their content) that are not owned by the publisher.

FaithWords books may be purchased in bulk for business, educational, or promotional use. For information, please contact your local bookseller or the Hachette Book Group Special Markets Department at special.markets@hbgusa.com.

Literary development: Lance Wubbels Literary Services, Bloomington, Minnesota.

Library of Congress Cataloging-in-Publication Data

ISBN: 9781546005377 (paper over board), 9781546005612 (ebook)

Printed in the United States of America

LSC-C

Printing 1, 2023

Contents

1

The Power of Believing

One of the greatest abilities God has given each of us is our ability to believe. If you believe, you can be successful. If you believe, you can overcome mistakes of the past. If you believe, you can fulfill your God-given destiny. There is incredible power in what we believe.

What you believe is greater than what the medical report says. We respect medical science, but God has the final say. When you get in agreement with God and believe what He says about you, what you believe can supersede any natural law.

What you believe is greater than what is in your bank account. I have a friend who came to the United States with nothing but the clothes on his back. Today, he runs a Fortune 500 company. Against all odds, he believed he could do what God put in his heart.

Activate the Greatness of His Power

The apostle Paul prayed in Ephesians 1:19 that those who believe would understand the incredible greatness of God's power. Notice the power is activated only when we believe. That means right now the Creator of the universe is just waiting to release healing, restoration, favor, promotion, and abundance. The only catch is that we have to believe.

Sometimes God will put a promise in your heart that seems impossible, a promise that says, "You will be healthy. You will start a business.

You will meet the right person and get married." It's easy to think, *It's never going to happen to me. I've been this way too long. I've made too many mistakes. The medical report is too bad. Nobody in my family has been successful.*

We can always come up with excuses. But instead of talking yourself out of it, just respond with three simple words: "Lord, I believe."

God says your children will be mighty in the land. "Lord, I believe."

God says He will restore the years that were stolen. He will bring you to a flourishing finish. "Lord, I believe."

God says whatever you touch will prosper and succeed. You will lend and not borrow, be the head and never the tail. Now, don't come up with five reasons why that will not happen. Your response should be: "Lord, I believe."

When you get in agreement with God, the incredible greatness of His power is activated.

Only Believe

In the Scripture, a man came to Jesus and said, "My little daughter is very sick. She is close to death. Will You come to my home and pray for her?" Jesus agreed, but along the way, He kept getting stopped, one interruption after another. Finally, word came back to Him saying, "No need to come. You've waited too long. The little girl has died."

The people were very distraught, but Jesus said to them, "Don't be afraid. If you will only believe, the little girl will be well."

Notice the phrase *only believe*. Jesus went to the home and prayed for the little girl, and she came back to life. You, too, may be facing situations that seem impossible. In the natural, you can't see how you could ever be healthy, how you could overcome the addiction, or how your family could ever be restored. But God is saying to you what He said to them: "If you will only believe, I will turn the situation around. If you only believe, breakthroughs are headed your way."

It's not complicated. God didn't say, "If you pray three hours a day" or "If you quote twelve chapters in the Scripture, I'll do it for you." No, He said, "If you will only believe." In other words, you just have to get your mind going in the right direction and believe you can rise higher. Believe you can overcome the obstacle. Believe your family can be restored. Believe you can do something great and make your mark in this generation.

When you believe, the surpassing greatness of God's power is released. You may have to develop new habits. If you've been negative for a long time, you will have to retrain your thinking from "I can't" to "I can." From "It won't happen" to "It will happen." From "I'll never get well" to "God is restoring health to me."

Don't Be Intimidated

First Chronicles 28:20 says you shouldn't be discouraged by the size of the task, for the Lord your God is with you. He will see to it that it is finished completely. When you believe, God will see to it that it's taken care of. When you believe, you have the Creator of the universe fighting your battles, arranging things in your favor, going before you, moving the wrong people out of the way. You couldn't have made it happen in your own strength, but because you are a believer, the surpassing greatness of God's power is at work in your life.

Now don't be intimidated by the size of the problem or the size of your dream. "Well, Joel, I was laid off, and you just don't know my financial situation." But I do know Jehovah Jireh, the Lord our provider. He is still on the throne. One touch of God's favor and you'll go from barely making it to having more than enough.

"Well, you just don't know my medical situation. It doesn't look good." But I do know Jehovah Rapha, the Lord our healer, has not lost His power. He has done it in the past. He can do it in the future.

"Well, Joel, I have big dreams, but I don't know the right people. I don't have the connections." That's okay. God does. You have friends in high places. When you believe, God will bring the right people across your path. Don't be intimidated by the size of what you are facing.

Here's what I've learned: The bigger the problem, the bigger your destiny. The enemy would not be fighting you this hard unless he knew God had something amazing in your future. On the other side of that challenge is a new level of your destiny.

No disappointment, no setback, no injustice, no person, no hater, and no jealousy can stand against our God. When you believe, all the forces of darkness cannot stop God from taking you where He wants you to go. Be a believer and not a doubter.

Discover Who He Is

It says in the book of Hebrews, "When we come to God we must believe that He is." It doesn't really finish the Scripture. Believe that He is *what*? The passage leaves it open-ended. This is saying that when you believe, God becomes whatever you need Him to be. He is strength when you're weak. He is healing when you're sick. He is favor when you need a good break. He is a way maker when you don't see a way. He is restoration when something has been stolen. He is vindication when you've been falsely accused. He is whatever you need Him to be.

You may know God by one name. You know Him as the Savior, and that's great. That's the most important way. But you need to find out what else He is. Do you know Him as a resurrection God, a God who can bring back to life what you thought was dead? Do you know Him as an Ephesians 3:20 God, a God "who is able to do exceedingly abundantly above all that we ask or think"? Do you know Him as a healer, a restorer, a God who gives beauty for ashes?

You may have endured hurts and disappointments, and people may have done you wrong, but you don't have to live defeated, depressed, in self-pity. God wants to heal the hurts, give you a new beginning, and bring you out better off than you were before. But you have to know Him as a God who gives beauty for ashes. There is so much more to our God. Don't keep Him in a box. Discover what else He is.

It Shall Be Well with You

A young couple who belong to Lakewood Church dreamed of buying their first home. For about a year and a half, they heard me talking about believing for Ephesians 3:20 and how God wants to show us His unprecedented favor. And they dared to believe. They let that seed take root. For the past ten years, they'd been working very hard and saving their funds so they could hopefully purchase a home.

At one point, everything came together. They found the house they liked. It was a good price. They had the money for the down payment, and they were so excited. But when they went to close on the home, there was a problem. The young lady was finalizing details at the real estate agent's office when her husband called. He said he had just been let go from his job. He had worked for that company for over six years. He always worked hard and had a good attitude, but his supervisor never particularly liked him. Over the years, his wife just kept encouraging him, "You're not working unto people. You're working unto God." He did his best to stay on the high road, but it seemed like at the worst possible time he was let go. To make matters worse, this all happened on his birthday. He lost his job and the house of their dreams on the same day.

They were very disappointed. But the good

news is that this young couple didn't just know God as a Savior. They knew Him as a God of restoration. They knew Him as a God of justice, a God who will make your wrongs right. They could have easily gotten bitter and dropped out of church, but they understood this principle: If you believe, you will see the goodness of God.

Instead of sitting at home every day depressed, in self-pity, the young man was either looking for a new job or at our church working as a volunteer week after week, month after month, as faithful as can be. In the natural, it didn't look as though anything was happening, but they weren't discouraged by the size of their problem. They knew that as long as they believed, the Lord their God would see to it that they were taken care of.

Five months after the husband was fired, he got a call from his old company. He hadn't talked to them since they let him go. It was an executive from the corporate headquarters. They had fired the old management team, and this new boss wanted him back. He not only restored his job but also restored all of his benefits, all of his retirement, and all of his seniority.

The house they'd wanted to buy had been sold by this time, but they found a better house in a better neighborhood for a better price. Today, the young husband has his job back, and they are living in their dream home. God is a faithful God.

Isaiah 3:10 says, "Say to the righteous, 'It shall be well with you.'" You may go through some difficulties. People may do you wrong. But because you're a believer, it shall be well with you. You lost your job, but another job is coming. It shall be well with you. The medical report doesn't look good, but we have another report: It shall be well with you.

You may have been praying and believing for your situation to change for a long time, but you don't see anything happening. Just as with the Lakewood couple, God is working behind the scenes right now arranging things in your favor. The answer is already on the way. It's just a matter of time before it shows up. It shall be well with you.

Set Your Thermostat

I like to think that having faith is like setting the temperature on a thermostat. You set the temperature to seventy-two degrees. Now it may be ninety-six degrees in the room, far off from where you set it. You could go to the thermostat and think, *This isn't working. It's not matching up.* Instead, you know it's just a matter of time before the air conditioning brings the temperature in the room down to match the temperature that you've set.

In the same way, we should set our thermostats on what God says about us. God says you will lend and not borrow. I'm setting my thermostat right there. That's what I'm choosing to believe. I may be far from that right now. I may be far in debt, but that's okay. I'm not worried. As long as I've set my thermostat, as long as I keep believing, keep honoring God, keep being my best, I know it's just a matter of time before the conditions in my life match up to the conditions in my thinking.

You may have a son who is at 140 degrees, out living wild. It doesn't matter. As long as your thermostat is set, you're not worried. You're not frustrated. You don't have to live wondering if he will change. You know God is in complete control.

God goes to work when He sees you have a made-up mind. Your thermostat is set on His promises, on faith, on restoration, on healing, on victory. It may not happen overnight, but God is faithful. He will do what He promised.

You may need to readjust your thermostat. At one time, you believed you would do something great. You believed you would start that business. You believed you'd beat that addiction. You believed you'd meet the right person and get married. But it didn't happen on your timetable. You grew discouraged, and you gave up.

God is saying, "Reset the thermostat." Start believing once again.

Believe you can live free from pain. Believe you can move into that nicer home. Believe God is bringing the right people across your path. Keep the thermostat set. Have a made-up mind.

When it gets cold or when it gets hot, stay in faith. Our attitude should be: *This is what God says about me. I am blessed. I will live and not die. My children will be mighty in the land. My latter days will be greater than my former days.*

You may not see anything happening week after week, month after month, maybe even year after year. It doesn't matter. Your attitude is: *My thermostat is set. I'm not moved by what I see, by what I feel, by what people tell me. I'm moved by what I know. And I know that when I believe, the incredible greatness of God's power is activated. I know that when I believe, strongholds are broken. Favor, healing, promotion, and restoration are coming my way.*

Do You Believe?

In the Scripture, the prophet Ezekiel was facing an impossible situation. There were dead bones in a valley. God had promised those bones would come back to life. Dead bones represent dreams and goals that we don't think will come to pass. God had the power to bring these dead bones to life, but God needed a person who believed so He could work through him.

God asked Ezekiel, "Do you believe that these dead bones can live?"

Isn't it interesting? God wanted to know what Ezekiel believed. Ezekiel could have reasoned it out and said, "God, the bones are dead. I don't see how that's going to happen."

In the same way, you could say, "The medical report doesn't look good, God. Business is slow. This is a big problem."

I can imagine God saying, "Ezekiel, I'm not asking you all of that. All I want to know is: Do you believe?"

All at once Ezekiel shook off the doubt, and he said, in effect, "Lord, I believe." Then the Spirit of God came on him. He started prophesying, and somehow, some way, those dead bones came back to life.

God is asking us what He asked Ezekiel. "Do you believe you can live a blessed, prosperous, successful life? I have the power. I'm just looking for someone who believes."

Do you believe God can turn that situation around? Do you believe you can overcome past mistakes? When you get in agreement with God and believe, that allows God to release the incredible greatness of His power.

"Even Now" Faith

In John 11, when Lazarus was very sick, his two sisters, Mary and Martha, sent word to Jesus and asked if He would come to their home in a different city and pray for Lazarus. But Jesus waited four days, which was too long. Lazarus had already died when Jesus finally showed up.

Martha was very upset. She said, "Jesus, if You had been here sooner, my brother would still be alive."

Have you ever felt God showed up too late for you? You prayed. You believed. But you still didn't get the promotion. You worked hard. You had a good attitude, but the company still let you go. You stood on God's promises. You quoted the Scriptures, but your prayers were not answered.

That was the way Mary and Martha felt. They were discouraged, depressed, and probably a little bit bitter. Jesus looked at them and said, "Take Me to the place where you have laid him." In other words, "Take Me to the place where you stopped believing. Take Me to the place where you decided it was over."

You have to go to that place in your life and ask yourself, "Is my God still on the throne? Is my God still all-powerful? Is my God still El Shaddai, the God who is more than enough?"

You have to stir up your faith. God said,

"Mary. Martha. It looks bad, but it's not over. If you will start believing once again, I will show you My power in a greater way."

Faith began to rise in their hearts. Martha said, "Jesus, if You would have been here, my brother would still be alive. But even now I know that whatever You ask of God, God will give it to You."

Sometimes you have to have "even now" faith where you say, "God, it looks impossible. It looks like it's over and done, but I know You are a supernatural God. I believe even now You can turn my finances around."

"Even now You can heal my body."

"Even now You can restore this relationship."

Mary and Martha shook off the doubt and started believing once again. You know the story: Jesus raised Lazarus from the dead.

Back in those days, the Sadducees, who were against Jesus, believed that the spirit left the body on the third day after a person died.

It wasn't a coincidence that Jesus waited for the fourth day to show up. He waited on purpose so that when He raised Lazarus there wouldn't be any doubt. They would know that it was a great miracle.

Sometimes God will wait on purpose, not only so you know that it's His power, but so your doubters, your naysayers, and your unbelieving relatives won't be able to deny that God has done something amazing in your life.

Moments before Jesus raised Lazarus from the dead, He said to Mary and Martha, "Did I not tell you if you would only believe you would see the glory of God?"

Mary and Martha at first were disappointed because Jesus didn't show up in time to heal Lazarus. They were disappointed that their prayers weren't answered in the way they wanted. But all along, God knew what He was doing. He wasn't planning a healing. He was planning something better. He was planning a resurrection.

Keep Believing

Just because you believed and it didn't work out your way or on your timetable doesn't mean that it's over. It means just the opposite. God is planning something better. You believed, but you didn't get the promotion. You believed, but you didn't qualify for the new home. Keep believing. God has something better coming.

You believed, but your child hasn't turned around. Keep believing. God will use your child in a great way.

You believed, but your year hasn't been that great so far. Keep believing. It's not over. God is still on the throne. Even now God can still turn it around.

Keep the thermostat set. Right now, behind the scenes God is working in your life, arranging things in your favor. Don't be intimidated by the size of what you are facing. Stay in faith, and the

Lord your God will make sure that it comes to pass.

Let this take root in your spirit. Because you are a believer, all will be well with you. All will be well with your family. All will be well with your finances. All will be well in your health. All will be well with your career. You need to get ready because God's promises are about to come to pass in your life.

It may not have happened in the past on your timetable. That's because God is not planning a healing. He is planning a resurrection. It will be better, bigger, and greater than you've ever imagined.

Be a believer. Take the limits off God. Keep your faith stirred up. I believe and declare you are going to see God's goodness in amazing ways!

2

Anchored to Hope

An anchor is usually a metal device that is attached to a ship or boat by a cable and cast overboard to hold the ship in a particular place. Once the captain arrives at his destination, he puts the anchor down. That way he won't drift and end up where he doesn't want to be. When the boat is anchored, it may move a little bit with the waves and the winds, but the captain is not worried. He can relax because he knows the anchor is down.

The Scripture tells us that hope is the anchor of our soul. What's going to keep your soul in the right place, what's going to cause you to overcome challenges and reach your dreams, is being anchored to hope. That means that no matter what you face, no matter how big the obstacle, no matter how long it's taking, you know God is still on the throne. You know His plans for you are for good, that He's bigger than any obstacle, and that His favor is surrounding you. When you are anchored to this hope, nothing can move you. The winds, the waves, and the dark storms of life may come, but you're not worried. You have your anchor down.

You receive a bad medical report, which would make most people upset and negative, but not you. You're anchored to hope. "I know that God is restoring health to me." You go through a loss or a disappointment, and your emotions are pulling you toward bitterness and depression. But there's something that's holding you back. You can't explain it, but deep down you hear that voice saying, "Everything is going to be all right. God has beauty for these ashes." That's the anchor of hope. Maybe your dream looks impossible.

You don't have the connections or the resources, and every voice says, "Give up! It's never going to happen. You're wasting your time." Most people would throw in the towel, but your attitude is: *I may not see a way, but I know God has a way. He's opening doors that no man can shut. Favor is in my future.* When you're anchored to hope, God will make things happen that you could never make happen.

I've learned that there will always be something trying to get us to pull up our anchor—bad breaks, delays, disappointments. In these tough times, when life doesn't make sense, when your prayers aren't answered, when it's taking longer than you thought it would, you have to make sure to keep your anchor down. If you pull it up, you'll drift over into doubt, discouragement, and self-pity. When you're anchored to hope, it's as though you're tied to it. You can't go very far. You may have thoughts of doubt that say, *This problem is never going to work out.* But your faith will kick in and say, "No, I know the answer is already on the way." On paper, it may tell you that it will take you thirty years to get out of debt. You could accept it, but because you're anchored to hope, there's something in you that says, "I know that God can accelerate it. I know that explosive blessings are coming my way." Your children may be off course, and it doesn't look as though they'll ever change. You could become discouraged, but you're tied to hope. Every time those negative thoughts come, trying to pull you away, your anchor kicks in. "As for me and my house, we will serve the Lord."

My question is: Do you have your anchor down? Do you have that hope, that expectancy that your dreams are coming to pass, that you're going to break that addiction, that your family is going to be restored? Or have you pulled up your anchor, and now you've drifted into doubt, mediocrity, not expecting anything good? Put your anchor back down. Scripture says, "Faith is the substance of things hoped for." You can't have faith if you don't first have hope. You have to believe that what God put in your heart will come to pass, that you will accomplish your dreams, that you'll meet the right people, that you'll live healthy and whole.

Be a Prisoner of Hope

One time, David had a lot coming against him. He felt overwhelmed by life. Everything just kept getting worse. He was down and discouraged and had given up on his dreams. He was stuck in a very dark place. But then he finally said, "Why are you cast down, O my soul? Hope in the Lord." He realized that he'd let his circumstances cause him to pull up his anchor of hope. He said, in effect, "I'm going to put my anchor back down. I'm going to hope in the Lord."

You may not see any reason to be hopeful, to keep believing. It doesn't look as though you'll ever get well, ever get married, or ever start that business. You have to do as David did and hope in the Lord. Don't put your hope in your circumstances; they may not work out the way you want. Don't put your hope in people; they may let you down. Don't put your hope in your career; things may change. Put your hope in the Lord, in the God who spoke worlds into existence, in the God who flung the stars into space. When you have your hope in Him, the Scripture says you'll never be disappointed. You may have some temporary setbacks. Life will happen, but when it's all said and done, you'll come out better than you were before.

The prophet Zechariah said it this way: "Return to your fortress, you prisoners of hope, and I will restore double what you lost." To be a "prisoner of hope" means you can't get away from it. You're anchored to it. You should be discouraged, but despite all that's come against you, you still believe as Joseph did that you're going to see your dream come to pass. You should be overwhelmed by the size of the obstacles you are facing. Goliath looked stronger and more powerful, but as with David, you have your hope in the Lord. You know that if God is for you, none will dare be against you. That sickness may seem as though it's going to be the end of you. You could be worried and feel stressed out, but you know nothing can snatch you out of God's hand. Your hope is not in the medicine, not in the treatment, not in the professionals, even though all those things are good and we're grateful for them. Your hope is in the Lord, in the God who breathed life into you. He's the God who makes blind eyes see. He's the God who caused a teenage shepherd boy to defeat a huge giant. He's the God who took Joseph from the darkness of the pit to the palace. He's the God who healed my mother of terminal cancer. I'm asking you to keep your anchor down. Keep your hope in the Lord.

When you find yourself being consumed by worry, full of doubt, thinking it's never going to work out, recognize what's happened. You've pulled your anchor up. The good news is that you can put it back down. Quit dwelling on the negative thoughts: *You'll never get well. You'll never get out of debt. You'll never meet the right person.* Turn it around and say, "Father, I thank You that the answer is on the way. Thank You that healing is coming, blessing is coming, freedom is coming, favor is coming, victory is coming." That's not just being positive; that's keeping your anchor down.

Hope On in Faith

This is what Abraham did. When God gave him a promise that he and his wife, Sarah, were going to have a baby, she was around seventy-five years old. It was impossible. It had never happened before. Abraham could have dismissed it and thought, *I must have heard God wrong.* I'm sure his friends said, "Abraham, you're an old man. Do you really think Sarah is going to have a baby at her age?" He could have talked himself out of it, but the Scripture says, "All human reason for hope being gone, Abraham hoped on in faith." Sometimes there's no logical reason to have hope. The medical report said that my mother would never get well. All the experts said that we'd never get the former Compaq Center for our church auditorium. Our opponents were much bigger and had more resources. There may be many reasons your situation will never work out. But you have to do as Abraham did—against all hope, hope on in faith. Don't pull your anchor up; don't get talked out of it. God is not limited by the natural. He's a supernatural God. Sarah was over ninety years old when she gave birth to a child. The promise was fulfilled, but they waited for fifteen years or so. It didn't happen overnight. There were plenty of times when they were tempted to think, *It's been too long. It's never going to happen. We're too old.* If they had believed those lies, they would have drifted into doubt and discouragement and never seen the promise come to pass.

Are you drifting into doubt, worry, and

negativity? I'm asking you to put your anchor down. Get your hopes up. Just because that promise hasn't been fulfilled yet doesn't mean it's not going to happen. You may have had some bad breaks as Joseph did, but that doesn't mean you're not going to fulfill your destiny. If it weren't going to work for your good, God wouldn't have allowed it. Shake off the self-pity, shake off the disappointment. What God promised you, He's still going to bring to pass.

A young lady who grew up in our church wanted to have a baby. She and her husband tried and tried and went through all the fertility treatments with no success. Year after year went by. When my father went to be with the Lord and I became pastor, she was the head of our children's department. At that time, she had already been believing to have a baby for over twenty years. We were in a meeting about the children's ministry, and she made the comment, "I have a good assistant trained because when I have my baby, I'm going to be out for a little while." I thought I had missed something. Nobody had told me that she was pregnant. I asked my sister Lisa afterward if this young lady was going to have a baby. She said, "No, she's just believing to have one." She talked as though the baby were already on the way. She didn't say, "If I have a baby." She said, "When I have my baby." What was that? She was anchored to hope.

I thought to myself, being the great man of faith who I am, *You've been believing for a baby for twenty years. It's time to move on. Maybe God wants to do it another way. Maybe you're supposed to adopt.* Don't let other people talk you out of what God put in your heart. Don't let them convince you to pull your anchor up. God didn't put the promise in them; He put the promise in you. That's why you can have faith when others think what you're believing for is far out. You can believe for it even though it seems impossible to them. This young lady kept her anchor down. Twenty-nine years after she started believing for a baby, she went to the doctor for a checkup. He said, "Congratulations, you're pregnant! And not with just one baby—you're pregnant with twins!" That's what Zechariah said: "If you stay anchored to hope, God will restore double what you lost." What you're believing for may be taking a long time, but what God started, He's going to finish. Keep your anchor down.

Everyday Life Can Cause You to Drift

When I was a little boy, our family would go to the beach in Galveston, Texas. I couldn't wait to get in the water and play in the waves. We'd find a place for our towels and shoes on the beach and then run out and start having fun in the water. After a couple of hours, we'd be ready to take a break, and when we looked around for our towels, we'd realize we were a couple hundred yards down the beach from where we'd started. We hadn't noticed that that whole time we had been slowly drifting. The Scripture describes hope as the anchor of our soul. It wouldn't say "anchor" unless there was a possibility of drifting. This is what happens in life. If we don't keep our anchor down and stay full of hope, then little by little we start drifting, getting negative and discouraged. "I don't think I'll ever have a baby. It's been so long." "I'll never get well." "I'll never meet the right person." The problem is that you don't have your anchor down.

When you're anchored to hope, you may have negative circumstances, but you're not worried because you know that God is fighting your battles. You may not see how your dream can come to pass, but you don't give up. You know that God is behind the scenes arranging things in your favor. You may have a disappointment, but you don't get bitter. You know that weeping may endure for a night, but joy is coming in the morning. *Anchored to hope* doesn't mean you won't have difficulties; it means that when those difficulties come, you won't drift. Nothing will move you. There will be waves, winds, and changing tides, but you're consistent—your hope is in the Lord.

What's interesting is that when we were at the beach, it wasn't a big storm or hurricane winds or huge waves that caused us to drift. It was just the normal movement of the ocean. If you don't have your anchor down, the normal currents of life will cause you to drift. To drift does not require a major sickness, a divorce, or a layoff; just everyday life will do it. Perhaps you don't realize it, but you have drifted into a dark place of doubt. You're not believing for your dreams anymore. You used to be excited about your dreams, but it's been so long that you've lost your passion. Maybe you've drifted into bitterness because you had a bad break or a person did you wrong. You used to be loving and kind, but now you're sour, not pleasant to be around. You used to believe that God was in control, knowing that He was taking care of you, but you pulled up your anchor, and you've drifted into worry. Now you feel stressed out all the time. The good news is that you can get back to where you're supposed to be. You can put that anchor of hope down and start believing again, start expecting His goodness and blessings.

Life is too short for you to go through it drifting, feeling negative, discouraged, and passionless. Get your hopes back up. If you don't have an expectancy in your spirit that something good is coming, it will limit what God can do. The apostle Paul told Timothy to stir up his gifts. You have to stir up the hope. If you don't, you'll drift into self-pity, worry, and discouragement. "Well, Joel, if God is good, why haven't my dreams come to pass? Why did I have this bad break?" Because you have an enemy who's trying to keep you from your destiny. But here's the key: The forces for you are greater than the forces against you. Don't let what happens to you, big or small, cause you to pull up your anchor. If you keep your hope in the Lord, God will get you to where you're supposed to be.

Cut Any Anchor of Negativity

This is not just about being positive. Being hopeful is about your soul being anchored to the right thing because if you're not anchored to hope, over time you'll become anchored to something else. You can become anchored to discouragement, where that's your default setting. You wake up discouraged and see everything with a tainted perspective. Everything is sour. It's because you're anchored to the wrong thing. I know people who are anchored to bitterness. They're so focused on who hurt them and what wasn't fair that bitterness has poisoned their whole lives. You can become anchored to self-pity and go around with a chip on your shoulder, always thinking about how unfair life has been. I'm not making light of what's happened. You may have a good reason to feel that way. I'm simply saying that being anchored to any of those things is going to keep you from your destiny. It's going to cause you to miss your purpose.

It's time to cut that anchor and come over into hope. God didn't breathe His life into you, crown you with favor, and give you a royal robe so you could go around anchored to doubt, fear, and bitterness. He created you to be anchored to hope, to go out each day expecting His goodness, believing that the days ahead are better than the days behind.

When you face difficulties, keep the right perspective. A difficulty is not there to defeat you; it's there to promote you. David could have looked at Goliath and thought, *Oh man, I'll never defeat him. He's twice my size. I don't have a chance.* If David had taken up his anchor of hope, we wouldn't be talking about him. Goliath wasn't sent to stop David; he was sent to promote David. What you're facing is not meant to hold you back; it's meant to push you forward. Instead of being negative and saying, "God, why is this happening? How is it ever going to work out?" stay anchored to hope. "God, I don't see a way, but my hope is in You. I know that You have it all figured out. You'll get me to where I'm supposed to be."

The Scripture says, "Hope deferred makes the heart sick." If you don't have hope that the problem is going to turn around, hope that the dream is going to work out, hope that the new house is in your future, or hope that your baby is on the way, then your heart, your spirit, is going to be sick. When you're not hopeful, positive, and expecting God's goodness, something is wrong inside. Even physically, when we feel stressed out and run-down, our immune system is weakened. It won't fight off disease as it should. For your health's sake, keep the anchor of hope down. We all go through seasons in life when things aren't exciting. It's easy to have the blahs and lose our enthusiasm. That's part of the normal currents of life. Nobody lives on cloud nine with everything perfect and exciting every day. Part of the good fight of faith is to stay hopeful in the dry seasons. When it's taking a long time, keep a smile on your face, and all through the day say, "Lord, thank You that You have good things in store." "Joel, what if I do that and nothing happens?" What if you do it and something does happen? I'd rather be anchored to hope than anchored to doubt, worry, and negativity. That's just going to draw in defeat.

One time a high school friend invited me to go fishing with him and his dad. We got in his boat and drove about an hour offshore and fished most of the morning. When we were finished, he asked me to pull the anchor up. I pulled and pulled and couldn't get it up. His father came over, and we pulled together, but it would not budge. My friend started the engine, a big powerful motor, and he started driving off very slowly, trying to force the anchor to come loose. It must have been caught under a big tree or rock because when he tried to pull away, it pulled the boat backward, and we almost tipped over. He circled the boat around to the other side and tried pulling it a different way, but the same thing happened. Finally, his father got his big knife out and said, "This is all we can do." He cut the line. We left the anchor in the ocean. My friend didn't like losing his anchor, but the alternative was to be stuck out in the gulf.

Sometimes we're anchored to things that don't come up easily. If you've been anchored to discouragement, anchored to worry, or anchored to negativity for a long time, you may have to do as my friend's dad did and cut the line, so to speak. The enemy doesn't want you to be free. He doesn't want you to be anchored to hope. He wants you to go through life feeling sour, discouraged, and doubting. It's time to cut some lines. It's time to say, "This is a new day. I've been anchored to this junk long enough. I'm done with the negativity and the bitterness, living passionlessly and with no expectancy. I'm cutting those lines, and I'm anchoring myself to hope." You have to have the right perspective when dark times linger. That sickness can't defeat you. That addiction is only temporary. The right breaks are in your future. You may have had some disappointments, and life may have dealt you a tough hand, but that cannot stop your destiny. The odds may be against you, but the Most High God is for you. When you're anchored to hope, He'll show out in your life in ways you've never imagined.

Keep Your Anchor Down

I know a young man named Owen whose family attends our church. At the age of thirteen, one of his favorite things to do was play basketball. He was always one of the best players on his team. His dream was to get a scholarship to play in college. He and his father were watching the 2014 NBA draft on television. There was a standout player from Baylor named Isaiah Austin who had been projected to go in the first round, but a few weeks before the draft, he'd learned that he had a life-threatening disease called Marfan syndrome. It's a genetic disorder that weakens the connective tissues of the body, with the most serious complications involving the tissue that holds the heart muscles and blood vessels together so the body can grow and develop. If it's not treated, it can easily be fatal. It's very dangerous to play high-energy sports if you have this syndrome. Isaiah Austin was given a ceremonial draft pick that night, and the commentators gave a lot of descriptive facts about his career-ending disease.

Owen's father recognized all the same symptoms in Owen. He took Owen to the doctor, and Owen was also diagnosed with Marfan syndrome and told he could never play basketball again. His body couldn't support it. Sometimes life doesn't seem fair. Owen could have cut the line to his anchor of hope, given up on his dream, and lived bitter and sour. But Owen knew that that disappointment wasn't a surprise to God. His father said that when Owen was told the diagnosis, he cried for thirty seconds, but then he said, "Dad, I'm only thirteen. I can still become a coach or a referee or maybe even work for the NBA." Then Owen decided he wanted to help other kids like him, so he started having fundraisers. In February 2016, he raised $140,000. I said that this young man needed to come work for us! Owen says, "You can make it your excuse, or you can make it your purpose."

Owen had to have open heart surgery, a very serious procedure, to fix valves in his heart that were much too large. If they kept growing, they would burst and cause instant death. One of the best surgeons for Marfan syndrome in the world lives here in Houston and operated on him. One day after the surgery, Owen was out of intensive care, and one week later, he left the hospital. One month later, he was back at church.

A bad break, a disappointment, a divorce, or a sickness can't stop you. When life throws you a curve, don't pull up your anchor. Do as Owen has done and keep hoping on in faith. You haven't seen your best days. God has you in the palms of His hands. It may have been meant for your harm, but He's going to use it for your good. If you stay anchored to hope, what is now your test will soon become your testimony. As with Owen, you will rise above every challenge, defeat every enemy, and become everything God created you to be.

3

By This Time Next Year

We all face challenges that look permanent, as if they'll never turn around, dreams and goals that seem as though they're a long way off. It's easy to get discouraged and accept that it's never going to work out. But what you can't see is God is working behind the scenes. What He promised you, He still has every intention of bringing to pass.

All the circumstances may say it's going to take years to get out of debt, years to meet the right person, but God is going to surprise you. It's going to happen sooner than it looks. There wasn't any sign of it. You weren't expecting it. Out of nowhere, your health improves, your business takes off, you break the addiction. Don't believe the lies that it's permanent. You may not see anything changing yet, but stay in faith; you are closer than you think.

It May Seem Too Good to Be True

In 2 Kings 4, there was a wealthy lady who lived in the town of Shunem. When the prophet Elisha came through, she would invite him to come to dinner with her and her husband. She could sense there was something special about Elisha. She told her husband, "He's a man of God. We need to take care of him." So she had a room built on top of her house, a guest suite so Elisha could stay there when he was in town. She could have just kept inviting him to dinner, which would have been nice. She could have rented him a room at the local inn, which would have been kind. But this lady went to great lengths to take care of Elisha. He had his own room on the roof of her house, with a beautiful bed, windows, and nice carpet.

One day Elisha was in town, resting in that bed. He began to think about how kind the lady was and how she'd gone to great expense to make sure he was comfortable. He said to his assistant, "Go ask her what she wants me to do for her. Ask if she wants me to put in a good word for her to the commander of the army." When he asked her, she said, "I don't need anything. We live in peace and security and don't need any special favors. We're blessed. We're healthy. Life is good." You might think Elisha would say, "Well, I tried my best. I'm glad this lady is blessed." But Elisha was determined to do something for her and didn't stop there. He asked his assistant, "What do you think I can do for her?" He said, "The only thing I can think of is that she's never had children. She's been barren her whole life, and her husband is old." Elisha said, "Call her. I want to speak to her." The lady came to the doorway, and Elisha said, "By this time next year, you're going to be holding a son in your arms." She nearly passed out. That was her dream. She said, "Sir, please, don't lie to me like that." Even though she thought it was too good to be true, even though she didn't really believe, a year later she gave birth to a healthy son. I could imagine that the bed she built for the prophet now held her little baby boy. She never dreamed that room she'd added to take care of the man of God would one day be used for her own child.

When you give to take care of God's work, when you're generous with your tithes and offerings as this lady was, God will always take care of you. You cannot give God something without Him giving you more back in return. This lady didn't need anything. She was blessed and happy, but God won't allow you to just be a giver. When you give, it will come back to you good measure, pressed down, and running over. This lady had already accepted that she couldn't have children.

It was too late. She had missed her window of opportunity, but God is not limited by the natural. He's a supernatural God. He can make things happen out of season.

What You Can't Buy

It may look as though you could never have a baby, never accomplish a dream, never get out of debt. God is saying to you what He said to the lady from Shunem, "By this time next year, you're going to see things happen that you never dreamed would happen." The medical report may not look good, but God can do what medicine cannot do. By this time next year, you could be cancer-free. You've been single a long time; get ready. By this time next year, you could be happily married. Business is slow; stay encouraged. By this time next year, you could be out of debt.

"Not me, Joel. You should see my finances." You should see my God. One touch of His favor will put you into overflow. When you read this, it can sound too good to be true. That's the way this lady felt. She said, in effect, "Elisha, don't get my hopes up. You know how long I've dreamed of having a baby." Her mind told her that it wasn't going to happen, but down in her spirit, something whispered, "This is for you. Receive it. Your baby is on the way." Your mind will tell you all the reasons why you won't get well or how you can't get out of debt, especially in a year. You think it's going to take thirty years. Your mind may say no, but if you listen down in your spirit, you will hear that still small voice saying, "Yes, it is on the way."

I talked to a lady who had a child born prematurely. Her son spent the first year of his life in the hospital. She had insurance, but it didn't cover the full amount. The part she owed was three million dollars, and while she was so grateful that her son was alive, she was a schoolteacher. It looked as though she would be paying on that debt for her whole life. But then she received a letter from the board of directors of the hospital that read: "We have decided to forgive your three-million-dollar debt." If that lady had read this chapter before she received the letter, she would have thought, *Joel, you have the wrong person. Me, out of debt in a year? That's not possible.* But if you asked her today, she would tell you that God can do the impossible. Just because you don't see a way doesn't mean God doesn't have a way. It's because He's going to do it out of the ordinary; it will be unusual; you won't see it coming.

Our part is to do as the Shunammite lady did in the Scripture and be a giver, have a generous spirit. When you're always being a blessing, God will make sure that you're always blessed. I don't mean just with material things. God can give you what money cannot buy. This lady already had wealth and influence, she knew the right people, but she didn't have children. God said to her, in effect, "I'm going to give you something you can't buy. Here's a son." God can bring you a divine connection, somebody in your life to love. You can't buy that. God can give you peace in your mind so you can lie down at night and sleep well. You can't purchase that. Perhaps you're fighting an illness. Every report says it's permanent, and you've been told to just learn to live with it. Receive this into your spirit: By this time next year, you're going to be healthy, whole, back on your feet, enjoying life. "Well, Joel, how could that be possible? The medical report says there's no way." There's another report: God says He is restoring health back to you. He says the number of your days, He will fulfill.

It's Going to Happen

I heard a story about a twelve-year-old girl who had a rare form of incurable cancer. Instead of going to school and playing with her friends, she spent her days in the hospital, very sick. It didn't look as though she would make it much longer. But some researchers received approval to use an experimental drug that they had never tried on people. She took the treatment, and after two months, the cancer started to shrink. Six months later, she was able to go back to school. At the age of fourteen, against all odds, she was cancer-free. But if you had told this young lady while she was in the hospital with terminal cancer, "By this time next year, you're going to be back at school with no cancer, full of energy, and enjoying life," she could have thought, *That's not possible. It's never happened with this type of cancer.* But God has the final say. You may think your marriage is beyond restoring, you've had the addiction so long you could never break it, you'll never get well, or you'll never meet the right person, but God is saying, "By this time next year, it's going to happen."

For dreams that look as though they'll take a lifetime to accomplish, get ready. It's going to happen sooner than you think. Things are about to fall into place. The right people are going to find you. Good breaks are going to track you down. You wouldn't be reading this if God wasn't about to do something amazing, something out of the ordinary. When we were trying to find property to build a new sanctuary, the doors kept closing. Everything fell through, and I didn't see any more options. I didn't think we could keep growing. It looked as if we were stuck. We didn't have any more room. Back then when I was so discouraged, if you had told me that by this time next year, we would have a building already built on the main freeway in Houston, one of the most recognized buildings in the city, the Compaq Center, I would have thought, *There's no way. How could that happen?* That was so far out of my thinking. But even though I couldn't fathom it didn't mean it didn't happen. Look where we are today.

Some of these things you may not be able to see yet. It seems too far out, so unlikely, but our God is so great that it doesn't mean it's going to keep Him from doing it. Because you honor Him, as this lady in the Scripture did, God is not only going to do more than you can imagine, but it's going to happen sooner than you think. It is not going to take your whole lifetime to accomplish the dream God put in your heart. By this time next year, you're going to be amazed at where you are. If you had told me when I was twenty-two years old and single, playing baseball every night and never really having dated anyone, that by that time next year, I would be engaged to a talented, fun, hot, fine, beautiful girl named Victoria, I wouldn't have believed it. But that didn't stop God from doing it. Thirty-six years later, we're still married, and I'm still just as good-looking—I mean, she's still just as good-looking.

God has some of these "by this time next year" moments lined up for you where you're going to look back and say, "Wow! I never dreamed I'd have this position, never dreamed my children would be doing this great, never dreamed I could build that orphanage." Get ready for God to show out in your life.

You Can't Dream This Up

When I was growing up, our family knew a very successful businessman who had built his company into a global brand that was known all over the world. His name was the company's name. He was very well respected and influential, but later in his career, the economy went down, and his business slowed. After years of being successful and seeing blessings, it looked as though he would end his career having to close his business with his reputation tarnished. He was in his late eighties and was millions of dollars in debt. It didn't look as though there was any way he could pay it. At his lowest moment when it looked so impossible, when he didn't think it could ever work out, he received a phone call out of the blue. An executive from another company said, "We'd like to purchase your company. We'll pay off all the debt. We'll renovate all the facilities, and we'll keep your name to honor your legacy."

That company spent over a hundred million dollars renovating its headquarters. Today that business is thriving more than ever. But if you had told this man in the middle of the downturn when it seemed so impossible that "by this time next year, you will not only be out of debt, but your business will be flourishing and your legacy will continue on," he couldn't have fathomed it. He never dreamed it would turn out that good.

As with this man, some of these things that seem so impossible, that seem so far out to you, by this time next year, you're going to be amazed. You couldn't make it happen. It is the hand of God on your life.

Think about Joseph, sitting in a prison for twelve years after having been betrayed by his brothers, sold into slavery, and then falsely accused of a crime by his master's wife—one bad break after another. There was nothing in his circumstances that looked as if he would ever accomplish his dream of ruling a nation. It looked just the opposite. If Joseph had heard me on the television or radio, he could have said, "Joel, I appreciate your encouragement, but I'm in prison. I'm a slave. I had no trial. I have no lawyer. I don't have anyone to stand up for me." He could have been discouraged. I believe that deep down Joseph could hear this still small voice saying, "This is not your destiny. Your time is coming."

One day the guard came over and told Joseph that Pharaoh wanted to see him. Joseph went in and interpreted Pharaoh's dream. Pharaoh was so impressed that he made Joseph the prime minister of Egypt. God has already lined up people in positions of influence who will open doors you couldn't open, bring you opportunities and promotion that you didn't see coming. As was true for Joseph, you don't have to find them, they will find you. But if you told Joseph while he was sitting in prison after over a decade of bad breaks and injustice that by this time next year, he was going to be second in command of the nation instead of being in prison, that he was going to be in charge, respected, and admired and have people serving him, he could have thought, *Are you kidding? Do you see these bars I'm behind?*

You may be in one of these unfair situations that seems as though it's never going to turn around. God is saying, "By this time next year, it's going to change. By this time next year, you're going to be vindicated, promoted, in a position of honor." Why are you worrying? Why are you losing sleep? God is still on the throne. He hasn't forgotten about you. Your time is coming. This looks like a stumbling block that you can't get past. The truth is, it's a stepping-stone that's about to take you to a new level of your destiny.

Get Your Hopes Up

In the Scripture, a man named Haman worked for the king of Persia. He had a very influential position, but he let it go to his head. All the people would bow down before him except for a Jewish man named Mordecai, who was a relative of Queen Esther. He knew it was only right to bow down before God. This made Haman so upset that he went to the king and said, "There's a group of people who don't obey your commands. They're troublemakers, and they need to be killed." He convinced the king to issue a decree that on a certain date all the Jews throughout the kingdom should be killed.

But one night the king couldn't sleep. He asked his assistant to bring him the book of the chronicles that recorded the history of his reign. The assistant brought the book and started reading accounts to the king at random. There just so happened to be a recording of how Mordecai had exposed a conspiracy to assassinate the king. The king was so impressed that the next morning he called Haman in and said, "Haman, what do you think we should do for a man whom I delight to honor and has never been recognized by the city?" Haman was so arrogant that he thought the king was talking about him, so he played it up really big. He said, "King, I think we should put a royal robe on him, have a big parade, and someone should march him on a horse up and down the streets while proclaiming what a great man he is." The king said, "I love that idea. Now go find Mordecai the Jew, and you do for him just what you said." It was an amazing setback and humiliation to Haman.

Meanwhile, Queen Esther set up a meeting with the king and Haman, and she exposed what Haman was really trying to do. Instead of getting rid of all the Jews, the king got rid of Haman. He sent out another decree that overruled the first decree, and he gave Mordecai the position Haman had occupied. If you had told Mordecai in the middle of the trouble, when it looked as though the Jews would be annihilated, that by this time next year Haman was going to be gone, the king's original decree was going to be overruled, and he was going to be in a position of honor, he could have thought, *That's too good to be true. How could all that possibly happen?* God has ways that we've never thought of.

You may be in a difficult situation, people are coming against you, your finances don't look good, there's trouble in a relationship. You could be upset and worried, but stay in peace. It is not permanent. As with Mordecai, by this time next year, it's all going to be turned in your favor. Because you honor God, He's dealing with those enemies. He's fighting your battles. Those people who are trying to stop you are not going to succeed. It looks as if they have the upper hand, they have more authority, and they may be over you, but the good news is that our God is over them. He controls the universe. Keep doing the right thing. Don't take matters into your own hands. Let God be your vindicator, and by this time next year, the enemies you see today you will see no more. By this time next year, what was meant for your harm will be turned to your advantage.

"Now, Joel, this is encouraging, but I don't see how it can happen for me." Neither did Mordecai, neither did Joseph, and neither did that twelve-year-old girl. You don't have to see how it can happen; all you have to do is believe. When you believe, angels go to work. When you believe, forces of darkness are pushed back. When you believe, things begin to change in your favor.

I talked to a man who had been in prison since he was seventeen years old. He was convicted of selling drugs and sentenced to forty years. He'd been watching our television broadcast in prison with the other inmates, and he'd given his life to Christ. He had a whole new outlook on his life. In one message, he heard me talk about how God is going to do things sooner than expected. That took root in his spirit. He started telling the other inmates that he was going to get out soon. They looked at him as if he wasn't all there. He had twenty-five more years left. Six months later, the warden called him in and said, "Because of good behavior, we're going to commute the rest of your sentence. You are free to go." The other prisoners looked at him as if to say, "Will you pray for us?" When he was released, the first place he came to was Lakewood. He flew here from another city.

When I met him, he had big tears running down his cheeks. He was so grateful, so overcome with emotion, he could hardly speak.

As with him, by this time next year, you're going to see things happen that you never dreamed would happen. By this time next year, you're going to be at a new level in your health, in your finances, in your career. By this time next year, you're going to be free from that addiction. God is up to something. He's about to show out in your life. "Well, Joel, you're just getting people's hopes up. I don't think this is going to happen for me." You're right; it's not going to happen. This is for people who believe. You have to let the seed take root. Here's the key: Don't talk yourself out of it. Talk yourself into it.

Sooner Than You Think

In 2 Kings 7, the Syrian army had surrounded the city of Samaria and cut off the Israelites' food supply. The people were starving and beyond desperate. It looked as though it was the end. The prophet Elisha showed up and said to the Israelites, "By this time tomorrow, there will be so much food that you can buy bread for a penny a loaf." People looked at Elisha as though he had lost his mind. They were surrounded, starving to death—it seemed impossible. One of the main leaders said, "Elisha, even if God opened the windows of Heaven, that still wouldn't happen."

There were four lepers sitting outside the city gates of Samaria. They said to one another, "We have nothing to lose. We're going to die anyway. Let's walk over to the enemy's camp and surrender. If they spare us, we live." They started walking toward the camp, and God multiplied the sound of their footsteps. The Syrians thought a huge army was coming to attack them. They panicked and took off running for their lives, leaving behind all their food, their supplies, and even their gold and silver. The lepers went back and told the Israelites, "It's just as Elisha said.

There is so much food that you could buy a loaf of bread for one penny."

"Joel, I thought you said by this time next year." Yes, but God also has some of these "by this time tomorrow" moments. It may not take a full year. God knows how to accelerate things. It's going to happen sooner than you think. You are closer than it looks. All the circumstances may say, "It's impossible. You could never get well that soon. Your business could never turn around overnight. You can't break the addiction by tomorrow. It's going to take years." You don't know what God is up to. You're looking at it in the natural. We serve a supernatural God. Don't be like that one leader in Samaria and think of all the reasons why it can't happen. Get in agreement with God. Believe something good is on the way. All through the day, thank Him that He's working in your life. If you do this, I believe and declare as Elisha did to the barren lady, "By this time next year, you're going to have your baby. That dream is going to come to pass. That problem is going to be resolved."

4

Ask Big

When God laid out the plan for your life, He didn't just put into it what you need to get by to survive, to endure until the end. He put more than enough in it. He's a God of abundance. We see this all through the Scripture. After Jesus multiplied the little boy's lunch of five loaves of bread and two fish, thousands of people ate, and yet there were twelve basketfuls of leftovers. It is interesting that they had counted the people beforehand, so Jesus knew how many people were in the crowd that day. If He had wanted to be exact, He could have made just enough so there would be no leftovers. On purpose, He made more than enough. That's the God we serve.

David said, "My cup runs over." He had an abundance, more than he needed. Yes, we should thank God that our needs are supplied. We should be grateful that we have enough, but don't settle there. That's not your destiny. He is a more-than-enough God. He wants you to have an abundance so you can be a blessing to those around you.

This is where the Israelites missed it. They had been in slavery for so many years that they became conditioned to not having enough, to barely getting by. When Pharaoh got upset with Moses, he told his foremen to have the Israelites make the same amount of bricks without the hay and straw being provided for them. I'm sure the Israelites prayed, "God, please, help us to make our quotas. God, please, help us to find the supplies that we need." They prayed from a slave mentality, from a limited mind-set. Instead of asking to be freed from their oppressors, they were asking to become better slaves. Instead of praying for what God promised them, the land flowing with milk and honey, they prayed that God would help them function better in their dysfunction.

Are you asking today to become a better slave, or are you asking for the abundant, overflowing, more-than-enough life that God has for you? God says you are to reign in life, that you are blessed and you cannot be cursed, that whatever you touch will prosper and succeed. Don't pray to just get by, to endure. Dare to ask big. Ask for what God has promised you. The medical report may not look good. That's okay. There's another report: "God, You said You would restore health to me. You said the number of my days, You will fulfill." Maybe you've gone through a disappointment, a bad break. Don't pray, "God, help me to deal with this loneliness. God, help me to put up with this depression." That's a slave mentality. Turn it around with some better thoughts: "God, You said You would give me beauty for these ashes, joy for this mourning, and that You would pay me back double for this unfair situation." Or your dream may look impossible. You don't see how it can work out: "God, You said Your blessings would chase me down, that I'm surrounded by favor, that goodness and mercy are following me, and that You would give me the desires of my heart."

Take the limits off God and ask big, not from a slave mentality, not from a limited mind-set. Don't ask God to help you function better in your dysfunction. Ask God to help you think bigger and better so you can live better. Ask Him for your dreams. Ask Him for new levels. Ask Him for explosive blessings. Ask Him to propel you into your purpose.

More Than Enough

This is what a lady I know did. She has four small grandchildren whom she ended up having to raise. She wasn't planning on it, but something happened with her daughter. At first, she was a little discouraged, not knowing how it was going to work out. Three of the children were in private school, which was very expensive, and the grandmother didn't have the extra funds to keep paying their tuition. She could've prayed from a slave mentality: "God, this isn't fair. I'll never be able to provide for my grandchildren. Please just help us to survive." Instead, she had the boldness to ask big. She said, "God, I don't have the funds to keep my grandchildren in private school, but I know You own it all. You're a God of abundance. And, God, I'm asking You to make a way, even though I don't see how it can ever happen."

At the end of the children's first school year, she owed a small amount on tuition, so she went to the school to pay. The secretary called up her records on the computer and said, "No, you don't owe anything. Everything's all paid up."

"That can't be," the grandmother responded.

"I have the notice right here. This says that I owe this amount."

The secretary turned the monitor around and said, "No, ma'am. It says right here that all three of the children's tuitions have been paid, not only for the rest of this year but all the way through the eighth grade." An anonymous donor had stepped up and prepaid the bills for years to come!

God can make things happen that you could never make happen. He's already placed abundance in your future. He's already lined up the right people, the breaks you need, doors to open that you could never open. My question is, Are you asking big? Or are you letting your circumstances—how you were raised, what somebody said—talk you out of it? If you go through life praying only "barely getting by" prayers, you'll miss the fullness of your destiny.

But when you get this in your spirit, that the God who breathed life into you, the God who called you, set you apart, and crowned you with favor, is a more-than-enough God, an abundant God, an overflowing God, you'll have a boldness to ask for big things. Those are power thoughts that will change how you live. You won't ask to just manage the addiction but to be free from the addiction. You won't ask to just pay your bills but to be totally out of debt so you can be a blessing to others. You won't ask to just see your child get back on the right course but that God will use him to make his mark on this generation.

What Is It That You Want?

The book of Matthew records the story of Jesus walking through a town where there were two blind men by the side of the road. When they heard all the commotion and that Jesus was passing by, they started shouting, "Jesus, have mercy on us!" Jesus walked over to them and said, "What is it that you want Me to do for you?" It seemed like a strange question. It was obvious what they needed. They were blind. Why did Jesus ask them? Because He wanted to see what they were believing. They could've said, "Jesus, we just need some help out here. We're blind. We just need a little better place to live or some cash for some food." If they had asked from a limited mentality, it would have kept them in defeat. Instead, they asked big. They said, "Lord, we want to see. We want our eyes to be opened." They were saying, "We know You can do the impossible." When Jesus heard their request, He touched their eyes, and instantly they could see.

God is asking us the same thing He asked those two blind men: "What is it that you want Me to do for you?" Now, how you answer is going to have a great impact on what God does. Don't say, "God, I just want to make it through this year. Have You seen what apartments are renting for these days?" "God, my family's so dysfunctional, just help us to survive." "God, I don't like my job. Just help me to endure it." That is going to limit your destiny.

Do what those blind men did. Dare to ask big. "God, I want to be free from this addiction." "God, I want to meet the right person." "God, I want to see my whole family serve You." "God, I want to start my own business." Ask for your dreams. Ask even for things that seem impossible. The Scripture says, "You ask and do not receive because you ask amiss." That word *amiss* in the original language means "sick, weak, miserable."

When we ask to become better slaves, that's a sick prayer. When we ask to get by, to endure, to barely make it, that's a weak prayer. That's asking amiss. God is saying, "I created the whole universe. I own it all. Don't come to Me with a sick prayer, a weak prayer, asking Me to help you live in mediocrity, endure the trouble, and survive another month. When you come to Me, ask big, knowing that I'm a God of more than enough." He's saying, "Ask Me to show out in your life. Ask Me to heal you from that disease. Ask Me to accelerate your goals."

When you ask big, God calls that a healthy prayer. That's when He says to the angels, "Go to work. Release My favor. Loose those chains. Open new doors." "Well, Joel, I'm just praying that I'll make it through these tough times. Business is really slow." May I say this respectfully? That's a sick prayer. That prayer has the flu! "I'm just praying that I'll learn how to manage this addiction. Grandmother had it. Mother had it. Now I do, too." That's a weak prayer. Your attitude should be: *God, this addiction keeps getting passed down through my family line, but I believe this is a new day and that You've raised me up to put a stop to it—that I will be the one to break the generational curse and start the generational blessing.*

Don't ask to become a better slave. Ask to be the difference maker. Ask to set a new standard. When you say, "God, help me to get that scholarship so I can go to college," that's not just being hopeful, just being positive. That's your faith being released. That's what allows God to do great things. Or, "God, I don't have the funds for the building project just yet. But, Lord, I want to thank You that opportunity is headed my way, that blessings are chasing me down." No more sick prayers. Take the limits off God. Ask big. This is the year for God to show out in your life, to accelerate His goodness, to propel you into your destiny.

No More Weak, Sick Prayers

This is what a man by the name of Jabez did in the Scripture. His name literally means "pain, sorrow, suffering." Every time someone said, "Hello, Jabez," they were saying, "Hello, Trouble." "Hello, Sorrow." "Hello, Pain." They were prophesying defeat and failure. You can imagine how he could have let that keep him in mediocrity, make him feel inferior and insecure. There was something different about Jabez, though. Despite his rough upbringing, despite what people labeled him, he looked up to the heavens and said, "God, I'm asking You to bless me indeed." He could have just said, "God, bless me." That would've been okay. But he had the boldness to ask big.

Jabez was a man who was supposed to have trouble and heartache, to live depressed and defeated, but he shook off the slave mentality. His attitude was: *It doesn't matter what people say about me. It doesn't matter what my circumstances look like. I know who I am—a child of the Most High God.* He went on to say, "God, enlarge my territories." He was saying, "God, help me to go beyond the norm. Let me see abundance. Let me see more of Your favor." I'm sure thoughts told him, *Jabez, God's not going to bless you. You come from the wrong family. Your own parents labeled you "sorrow, pain, trouble."* But people don't determine your destiny; God does. The Scripture says that God granted Jabez his request. God blessed him indeed.

As with Jabez, you may have plenty of reasons to settle where you are—what you didn't get, what people said, how impossible it looks. The odds may be against you, but the good news is that God is for you. He is more powerful than any force that's trying to stop you. He knows how to make up for what you didn't get. He can thrust you further than you ever imagined, but you have to do as Jabez did and pray bold prayers. Ask in spite of what the circumstances look like. Ask in spite of what people are telling you. Ask in spite of what the enemy keeps whispering in your ear.

Jabez could have prayed a weak, sick prayer and thought, *God, I've had some bad breaks. I had a rough upbringing. I'm just asking You to help me survive.* If he had done that, we wouldn't be talking about him today. If you're going to beat the odds, stand out in the crowd, and reach your highest potential, you have to learn this principle of asking big.

Today Is Your Birthday

God says in Psalm 2, from *The Message* transla-
tion, "You're my son, and today is your birthday. What do you want? Name it: Nations as a
present? Continents as a prize? You can command them all to dance for you." Notice how
big God thinks. Sometimes we're praying for a
three-dollar-an-hour raise; God's talking about
giving you nations. We're praying for a promotion; God's got a business for you to own. We're
praying to pay our bills; God's planning on blessing you so you can pay other people's bills. We're
looking at the five loaves and two fish; God's
thinking about the twelve basketfuls of leftovers.

What does that mean, "Today is your birthday"? On your birthday, more than at any other
time, you feel entitled to ask for something out
of the ordinary. Normally, you don't want any-
body to go out of the way for you, but on your

birthday, you think, *Okay, I'm going to ask for a new ring or for a set of golf clubs.* Over time, as we get older, our enthusiasm may go down a little, but think back to when you were a child. You knew that was your special day. You had the boldness to ask for what you really wanted.

A while ago, a little boy came up to me out in the hallway. He's five years old, and I see him at the church all the time. He came running up, so excited, and exclaimed, "It's my birthday today!" I gave him a big hug and told him, "Happy birthday!" I walked about five steps away, and he came back and grabbed my leg and said it again: "It's my birthday!" I thought, *I know, you just told me five seconds ago.* We hugged and did it all again as though it was the first time. This happened again and again and again. I could hardly get through the hallway. About the seventh time, he came up and grabbed my leg. This time, instead of telling me it was his birthday, he looked up and said, "What are you going to get me for my birthday?" The reason he kept coming back is because he felt entitled to a present. He knew it was his special day.

God is saying, "When you pray, act as though it's your birthday. Come to Me with a boldness. Ask Me for what you really want. Don't be shy. Don't hold back. Tell Me your dreams. Tell Me what you're believing for. Ask for the secret things I placed in your heart."

When our son, Jonathan, was a little boy, he liked the little action figures of the Power Rangers. He never asked for that much, but on his sixth birthday, he said, "Dad, I really want that new Power Ranger I saw on television." We drove to the closest toy store, but they were sold out of that Power Ranger. We drove to another store, and they didn't have it—and another, and another, and another. Normally, I would've given up, but it was my son's birthday. I didn't want to disappoint him. Finally, we found one at a toy store an hour away. It took half the day to get this little fourteen-dollar action figure. But as a father, I didn't mind going out of my way.

You know how, as parents, you'll do anything for your children, especially on their birthday. How much more will your Heavenly Father make things happen for you? Ask Him for your dreams. Ask Him to turn your child around. Ask Him for your healing. You're not inconveniencing God. "Well, Joel, God has bigger things to deal with than me." No, you are God's biggest deal. You're the apple of His eye. You're His most prized possession. Just like I ran all over the city to find that action figure to give my son what he was dreaming of on his birthday, God will move Heaven and Earth to bring about His destiny in your life. Dare to ask big.

It Is Your Father's Good Pleasure

Too often, instead of approaching God as though it's our birthday, believing that He'll do something special, we do just the opposite. "Joel, I can't ask for what I really want. That wouldn't be right. That would be greedy. That would be selfish." The Scripture says it is the Father's good pleasure to give you the kingdom. Nothing makes God happier than for Him to see you step up to who you were created to be. Psalm 2 says, "Today is your birthday. What do you want?" Notice, today is always in the present. When you get up tomorrow morning, God is saying, "Today is your birthday." Two weeks from now, "Today is your birthday." Seven years from now, "Today is your birthday." Every morning when you get up, just imagine God saying, "Happy birthday, Son." "Happy birthday, Daughter." Why does He do this? So you'll have the boldness to ask for things that you wouldn't normally ask for.

When I received word that the Compaq Center was coming available, something ignited inside me. I knew it was supposed to be our church auditorium, but every voice said, "It's never going to happen. It's too big, Joel. You don't deserve it. Who do you think you are to even ask for it?" Instead of believing those lies, I did what I'm asking you to do. I went to God as though it was my birthday, and I said, "God, I know this is far out. Normally, I'd never ask for it, but, God, I believe You put this in our path. This is part of my destiny. So, God, I'm asking You to make a way, even though I don't see a way."

What is interesting is that in all the big things I've ever asked God for, I've never once felt as though He said, "Joel, you've got a lot of nerve. What are you doing, asking for that?" Just the opposite. In my heart, I can feel God whispering, "Joel, I love the fact that you dare to ask big. I love the fact that you believe I can do the impossible." Of course, everything I've asked for hasn't come to pass, but the point is, if you go to God with childlike faith, believing that it's your birthday, asking for things that you wouldn't normally ask for, there will be times when you see God show out in your life in ways greater than you ever imagined.

Stand Out and Make a Difference

This is what King Solomon did. In Psalm 72, he prayed what seemed to be a very self-centered prayer. He asked God to make him well-known, that his fame would spread throughout the land, that the wealth and honor of other nations would be brought to him, and that kings and queens would bow down before him. You would think God would say, "Solomon, what's wrong with you? I'm not going to make you famous. I'm not going to give you this honor, wealth, and influence. You need to learn some humility." But God didn't rebuke him. God didn't tell him he was selfish and greedy. God did exactly what he asked for. Solomon became one of the most famous people of his day. The queen of Sheba came, bowed down before him, and brought him gold and silver.

Here's the key: The reason God answered that bold prayer is because Solomon went on to pray,

"God, if You make my name famous, if You give me influence and wealth, I will use it to help the widows, to take care of the orphans, to bring justice to the oppressed, to give a voice to those who don't have any voice." He asked big, not just so he would look impressive, drive the fanciest chariot, and live in the biggest palace. It was so he could lift the fallen, restore the broken, and help the hurting to advance God's kingdom. God has no problem giving you influence, honor, wealth, and even fame, as long as your dream, in some way, is connected to helping others, to making this world a better place. When your thoughts align with God's thoughts for others, He will help make your life better.

God is raising up a new generation of Solomons, people who have the boldness to say, "God, make me famous in my field. Let my gifts and talents stand out. Let my work be so excellent, so inspiring, that people all around me know who I am, not for my glory but so I can use my influence to advance Your kingdom." Whatever field you're in—medicine, sales, construction, accounting, teaching—I dare you to pray, "God, make me famous in my field. Let me shine. Give me influence."

If you're an architect, dare to pray, "God, give me ideas, creativity, and designs that stand out." Then use your influence to design a boys' home or an orphanage.

If you're a mechanic, dare to pray, "God, make me famous. Let me be so skilled and have so much expertise that people come to me to see how it's done." Then use your influence to fix the cars of single moms, to mentor young men and teach them how to do it.

If you're in the medical profession, dare to pray, "God, make me famous. Let me develop procedures that benefit mankind." Then use that influence to help those who can't afford treatment. There's no limit to what God will do for you if you use what He's given you to help others.

One time, I was playing basketball with some friends, and I had to leave early to go to a doctor's appointment. A teammate of mine works in the medical field, and he asked me who I was going to see. I said, "Dr. Price, a friend of mine."

He looked up and said, "*The* Dr. Price?"

"No, *just* Dr. Price," I replied. "I've known him for thirty years."

"Is he *the* Dr. Price who's in infectious medicine?"

"Yes, that's him," I said.

"Oh, man," he exclaimed, "he's the best! He's famous. People come to see him from all over."

It's interesting that Dr. Price uses his "fame," his wealth, and his influence to help provide needy people in third-world countries with free medical supplies, vaccinations, and antibiotics. Dr. Price never dreamed he would be where he is today or that his medical mission organization, International Medical Outreach, would treat over fifty million children in twenty-one countries. God made him famous—not TMZ famous, but famous in his field.

I wonder what would happen if you would

dare to pray, "God, make me famous. God, cause me to stand out so I can make a big difference in this world." God can make things happen that you could never make happen. He'll cause you to stand out so you can use your influence not only to reach your goals but so you can help others along the way.

Now do your part. No more sick prayers. No more weak prayers. Get rid of that slave mentality. Go to God as though it's your birthday. Ask Him for your dreams. As Jabez did, dare to say, "God, bless me indeed." If you do this, I believe and declare, as He did for Solomon, God is going to give you more influence, more resources, and more notoriety. The greatness in you is about to come out, with new levels of favor, abundance, and purpose.

5

Step Into the Unknown

When I type an address into my navigation system, one of the options that comes up is "Route Overview." When I click on that, it gives me all the details of my trip. There may be fifteen different instructions. "Travel six miles on the highway, get off at Exit 43, go four hundred feet, turn left at the intersection." Your whole route is clearly laid out. You know where you're going, how long it's going to take, and what to expect. Knowing all the details makes us comfortable. We can relax.

In a similar way, God has a route overview for

your life. Before you were formed in your mother's womb, He laid out your plan. He not only knows your final destination, He knows the best way to get you there. But unlike the navigation system, God doesn't show you the route overview. He doesn't tell you how it's going to happen, how long it's going to take, where the funds are going to come from, or whom you're going to meet. He leads you one step at a time. If you trust Him and take that step into the unknown, not knowing how it's going to work out, He'll show you another step. Step by step, He'll lead you into your destiny.

The difficulty of this method is that we like details. We wouldn't have any problem with taking that step of faith—starting that business, going back to school, moving to that new location—if we knew where the money was coming from, how long it was going to take, and that the right people were going to be there for us. If we had the details, it would be easy to step out. But here's the key: God doesn't give the details.

He's not going to give you a blueprint for your whole life. If you had all the facts, you wouldn't need any faith. He's going to send you out not knowing everything. If you have the courage to step into the unknown and do what you know He's asking you to do, doors will open that you could never have opened, the right people will show up, you'll have the funds and any other resources you need.

The Scripture says, "Your word is a lamp to my feet and a light to my path." "A lamp" implies you have enough light to see right in front of you. He's not giving you the light that shows your life for the next fifty years. It's more like the headlights of a car. When you're driving at night with your low-beam headlights, you can only see a hundred feet or so in front of you. You don't stop driving because you can't see your destination, which is twenty-five miles ahead. You just keep going, seeing as much as the lights allow, knowing you'll eventually arrive at your destination.

My question is: Will you believe and take the

next step that God gives you with the light you have? If you're waiting for all the details, you'll be waiting your whole life. We all want to be comfortable, but walking in God's perfect will is going to make you a little uncomfortable. There's a healthy tension: You have to stretch, you have to pray, and you have to believe. You're not going to be sure how it's all going to work out, but that is what will cause you to grow, that's when you'll learn to trust God in a greater way. God is not interested only in the destination. He's teaching you along the way. He's getting you prepared and growing you up. He will lead you purposefully into situations where you're in over your head, your friends can't help you, and you don't have the experience you think you need. Too often we shrink back and think, *I'm not going there. I'm not qualified. I'm too nervous. What if it doesn't work out?* God knew that you would be nervous, and He knew that you would feel unqualified. That's a test.

Are you going to talk yourself out of it? Are

you going to let the fear of what you can't see hold you back? Or are you going to be bold and step into the unknown? The unknown is where miracles happen. The unknown is where you discover abilities that you never knew you had. The unknown is where you'll accomplish more than you ever dreamed. Just because you don't have the details doesn't mean God doesn't have the details. He has the route overview for your whole life. He wouldn't be leading you there if He didn't have a purpose. He has the provision, He has the favor, and He has what you need to go to the next level.

You Have to Be Bold

One thing I like about my navigation system is that it gives me specific details. "Go 9.3 miles down this freeway and exit at...." The whole time it counts down—eight miles left, seven miles, six miles. It's all right in front of me to see.

But God does not direct us that way. He'll tell you to go down a certain road. Then the first thing we do is ask for details. "How far do You want me to go?" No answer. "Where do You want me to turn?" No answer. "Who's going to meet me?" No answer. It would be so much easier if God would give us specifics. But that wouldn't take any faith. Can you endure the silence of not knowing everything? Will you trust God even though you don't have the details? Will you take that step of faith even though you're nervous, uncomfortable, and not sure how it's going to work out?

This is what Abraham did. God told him to leave the place where he was living and go to a land He would show him. Abraham was to pack up his household, leave his extended family behind, and head out to a land that God was going to give him as his inheritance. The only problem was that God didn't give him any details. The Scripture says, "Abraham went out, not knowing where he was going." I can imagine

Abraham telling his wife, Sarah, "Honey, I have great news. We're going to move. God promised me He's taking us to a better land where we're going to be blessed in a new way." I can hear Sarah saying, "That's so exciting! I can't wait. Where are we going?" Abraham answers, "I'm not sure. He didn't tell me." She asks, "What should I wear? Will it be hot or cold?" He answers, "I don't know." At that point, reality sets in for Sarah, who responds, "Well, Abraham, how are we going to make a living? Where are we going to get food for our children and staff? This seems like a mistake. Are you sure that God told you this?"

If you're going to step into the unknown, it's going to take boldness. It's not always going to make sense. Other people may not understand. They may try to talk you out of it. Your own thoughts will tell you, *You better play it safe. This is too big a risk. What if it doesn't work out?* Abraham understood this principle. He knew that just because you don't have all the answers and just because you're nervous and uncomfortable doesn't mean you aren't supposed to do it. The psalmist says, "The steps of a good person are ordered by the Lord." If you take that step, not knowing all the details but trusting that God knows what He's doing, then each step of the way there will be provision, there will be favor, there will be protection. Yes, it's uncomfortable not knowing the details, and, yes, you have to believe, you have to pray, and you have to trust. But every step you'll not only have God's blessing, you'll also be growing and getting stronger.

It Is Possible to Walk on the Water

In the Scripture, when Jesus came walking across the stormy sea in the darkness of night, Peter was the only disciple to walk on the water to Him. He also was the only one who had the courage to get out of the boat in the first place. I can imagine the other disciples saying, "Peter, you better stay

in here with us! The waves are big. It's too dangerous. You could drown." But when Jesus told him
to come, Peter stepped out into the unknown
and walked on the water. "Well, Joel, you failed
to note that he sank." Yes, but he walked on the
water more than you or I have. Although what
is familiar is comfortable, it can become a curse
rather than a blessing. Familiarity—what you're
used to, how you were raised, the job you've
had for years—can keep you from your destiny.
Don't let your comfort keep you from getting out
of the boat and becoming who you were created
to be.

If Abraham had put his comfort above fulfilling his purpose, we wouldn't be talking about
him. It was a risk to pack up his family and leave,
not knowing where he was going. You can't play
it safe your whole life and reach the fullness of
your destiny. Don't let the what-ifs talk you out of
it. "What if I fail? What if I don't have the funds?
What if they say no?" You'll never know unless
you try. When you come to the end of your life,

will you have more regrets about the risks you took or about the risks you didn't take? "What if I start a new business and it fails?" What if you start it and it thrusts you to a new level? "What if I get into this new relationship and I get hurt again?" What if you get into it and you're happier than you've ever been? What if it's a divine connection? "What if I take this new position and I'm not good at it? What if I'm not successful?" What if you take it and you excel? What if you discover new gifts you didn't know you had? What if it leads you to more opportunities?

For every major victory and every significant accomplishment in my life, I've had to step into the unknown. When my father went to be with the Lord and I stepped up to pastor the church, I didn't know how it was going to work out. I didn't know if I could minister. I didn't know if anyone would listen to me. Every voice said, "Don't do it! You're making a mistake. You're going to get up there and look like a fool." I knew I was going in over my head, and I knew I didn't have the experience. But I also knew that when we are weak, God's power shows up the greatest. I couldn't see very far down the road. I couldn't see anything of what we're doing today. All I could see was this much: "Joel, step up and pastor the church." If God had shown me all that we're doing today and what it would take to get here, I would have said, "No way. I can't do that." Sometimes the reason God doesn't tell us what's in our future is that He knows we can't handle it right then.

What God has in store for you is going to boggle your mind—the places He's going to take you, the people you're going to influence, the dreams you're going to accomplish. It's going to be bigger than you've imagined. You know where it is—it's in the unknown, in what you can't see right now, in what you don't feel qualified for, in what looks way over your head. When you have something in front of you that seems too big and you don't think you have what it takes to do it, that's God stretching you. He sees things in you that you can't see. You may be uncomfortable, but don't shrink back. Keep stretching, keep praying, and keep believing. You're growing. God is leading you step by step. You are about to step into the next level. You've been on that step you're on for long enough. You've passed that test, and now the next step is coming—a new level of favor, a new level of blessing, a new level of influence, a new level of anointing.

Take the Step of Faith

Victoria and I were driving to another city a while ago. I had my navigation system on. At one point, we were on a country road for about a hundred-mile stretch. There were so many intersections where roads veered off from it. I was concerned that I had missed my turn. I had to keep looking to make sure that I was okay. I noticed that as long as I was on the right path, the voice of the GPS was silent. I wished she would come on and say, "You're doing good. Keep going. You're right on track." But she never said a thing until it was time to do something different. Sometimes God is silent. You don't hear Him saying anything. It's easy to think you must be off course, something must be wrong. He's not talking. But as with the GPS, that means you're on the right course. Keep being your best with what you have. Keep stretching, praying, and believing. The next step is coming. You have to pass the test of being faithful where you are. That next step is going to be an increase step, a favor step, a healing step, a breakthrough step.

In the Scripture, when Joshua and the Israelites came to the Jordan River, there was no way for them to get across. The people had heard how Moses had held up his rod and the Red Sea had parted many years before. I'm sure that Joshua thought that if he did the same thing, the waters would part for him. But God had a different plan. He told Joshua to have the priests who were carrying the ark of the covenant step into the river, and then the waters of the Jordan would part. I can imagine the priests saying, "Joshua, you want us to walk into the water? That doesn't make sense. We could drown in those dark waters." They got to the shore and nothing happened. They got to the banks a few feet away and still nothing. Thoughts started telling them, *What if it doesn't part? What if Joshua made a mistake? What if we get out there and can't get back?* They could have talked themselves out of it, but instead they dared to step into the unknown. The Scripture says that the moment their feet touched the edge of the waters, the water upstream began piling up while the water on the other side flowed downstream. It wasn't long till the riverbed was empty and they were able to walk across on dry land.

Notice that the miracle happened along the way. We think, *God, when You part the river, I'll go.* God says, "Go, and I'll part the river." If you step into the unknown, along the way you'll see miracles, doors will open that you couldn't open, and the right people will show up. God could have just as easily parted the water first, before the priests stepped in. He was showing them and us this principle: When you don't see how it can work out, when you don't know where the funds are coming from, when every thought tells you to play it safe, but you take that step of faith and do what God has put in your heart, you're showing God that you trust Him. That's when Jordan Rivers will part. God will purposefully put us in situations where we can't do it on our own and it looks impossible—that's a test of our faith. If you stay in the boat, you'll never walk on the water. You'll never see the fullness of your destiny. If God had parted the water before the Israelites stepped into it, it would have been a lot less stressful. They wouldn't have had to pray and believe and stretch. But here's the key: God uses the journey to get us prepared for where we're going. When we have to stretch our faith, believe that He's making a way, and thank Him that things are turning in our favor, that is strengthening our spiritual muscles. We're developing a greater confidence in God.

The Purpose Is to Prepare You

When I received word that the former Compaq Center was coming available, I didn't know how complicated it would be to acquire it for our church auditorium. I had to step into the unknown. It was a city-owned facility. The mayor was a friend of our family. I called him, and he was in favor of our purchasing it. That was the first miracle. We needed ten votes from city council members, and we had only nine, but the night before the main vote, after two years of opposing us, a council member changed his mind and decided to vote for us. We got the building! Another miracle. A week later, however, a company filed a lawsuit to try to prevent us from moving in. We were told that it could be tied up in the courts for up to ten years. I had already told the church the building was going to be ours, and people had given money. I would wake up in the dark of night sweating, with thoughts telling me, *This is going to be a big mess. You're going to look like a fool. You have to give those funds back.* But as happened for Joshua, along the way miracles kept happening. The CEO of that opposing company eventually flew in from out of town. Our lawyers told us it was a ploy to try to confuse things, but he said, "Joel, I watch you on television, and my son-in-law is a youth pastor. Let's work something out." Two days later, the lawsuit was dropped. We were on our way. When you go out not knowing where you're going, God will make things happen that you could never make happen. You'll see Jordan Rivers part, you'll see Compaq Centers fall into place, you'll see the surpassing greatness of God's favor. Don't stay in the boat. Don't let the fact that you can't see all the details hold you back. You're not supposed to see it all. God is leading you step by step.

When you're in the unknown, when you're stretching, praying, and believing, that's when you're really growing. The journey is more important than the destination. Why? Because if you're not prepared during the journey, if you don't learn what you're supposed to learn along the way, you won't be able to handle where God is taking you. God could have given us the Compaq Center in the first week we prayed, or at least the first month. That would have saved me a lot of stress, a lot of praying, and a lot of believing. Why did He wait three years? He was getting me prepared. I was learning to trust Him, my faith was being increased, and my character was being developed.

It's interesting that during those three years, as with the silence of the lady who voices the GPS, I didn't hear anything new. I didn't hear God say,

"You're doing good, Joel. Be patient. It's all going to work out. I've got you covered." I had to trust Him when He was silent. I had to believe that He was in control even when I didn't see any sign of it. I had to keep reminding myself that the steps of a good person are ordered by the Lord. I took my steps knowing that God had put the dream in my heart. I didn't know how it would work out. I didn't know if we would be successful, but I believed that I was doing what God wanted us to do.

Here's the thing: Even if you miss it, even if it doesn't work out the way you thought, God knows how to use it for your good. God would rather you take a step of faith and miss it every once in a while than play it safe all the time and never make a mistake. Sometimes the mistakes, the closed doors, and the times we miss it are parts of God's plan. They're preparing us for the next open door. But if you're concerned that you're going to miss the next step, you'll never get off dead center.

The Not-Knowing Factor

Too many times we let the fear of the unknown hold us back. When you're in God's will, there's going to be a not-knowing factor. You're not going to know all the details about how it's going to work out or where the funds are going to come from. If you're going to reach your highest potential, you have to have the boldness to step into the unknown.

My brother, Paul, is a medical doctor. For seventeen years, he was the chief of surgery at a hospital in Arkansas and had a very successful practice. It looked as though that's how he would spend his life. But when my father went to be with the Lord in 1999, my brother felt God leading him to come back and help us pastor the church. His colleagues told him that he was having a midlife crisis. They said that he should wait a couple of years in order to get over our father's death and not make an emotional decision. But deep down Paul knew what he was supposed to do, even though leaving his medical practice and all that training didn't make sense to his mind. Thoughts asked him, *What if it doesn't work out? What if you don't like it? What if they don't like you? What if you get back there and Joel makes fun of you?* In the natural, it looked as though he were making a mistake, but as Abraham did, Paul went out, not knowing how it was going to work out. He didn't have all the details. We didn't come up with a ten-year strategy. All he knew was that first step: "Go help your family."

What Paul didn't know was how the ministry was going to grow. He didn't know that after eight years of his being faithful in the pastoring of the church, God would open the door for him to go to Africa for several months a year and operate on people. Paul's dream had been to do medical missions, but he'd thought he was giving up medicine completely. What he couldn't see was that it was all a part of God's plan. If he hadn't stepped into the unknown, he wouldn't have reached the fullness of his destiny. When you have the boldness to go out, not knowing all the details, your life will be more rewarding and more fulfilling than you ever imagined.

Be Like Esther

In Chapter 3, I mentioned that there was a young Jewish girl in the Scripture named Esther. She was an orphan, didn't come from an influential family, and was living in a foreign country. But God raised her up to become the queen, and now she was living in the palace. There was a powerful official who was able to pass a law that all the Jewish people be killed. Esther's uncle Mordecai told her of the decree and said that she had to go in and plead with the king for their people. In those days, if you approached the king without his holding up his golden rod first, you would be killed. She said, "Mordecai, I can't just go in there. What if he doesn't hold it up? That will be the end of me." God was asking her to step into the unknown, but the what-ifs started coming. "What if the king is offended, gets upset, and doesn't hold it up? I'll be dead." She was about to talk herself out of it. But Mordecai said, "Esther, if you keep silent, deliverance for the Jews will come from someone else, but you and your family will perish. Who knows but that you have come to the kingdom for such a time as this?" God was saying, "Esther, if you don't do it, I'll find somebody else. But the problem is that you're going to miss your destiny." This opportunity wasn't going to come again. This was her chance to make her mark. It was now or never. I love what Esther did. She rose up and said, "I will go before the king, which is against the law; and if I perish, I perish! But I will not let this moment pass." She stepped up, and not only did God give her favor with the king, but she saved her people and became one of the heroes of faith.

As with Esther, we all have opportunities that are not going to come our way again. When my father died and I had to make that choice to step up or play it safe, that was one of those now-or-never moments. When they come your way, don't shrink back, don't let fear talk you out of it, and don't let the what-ifs keep you in your boat. Do as Esther did. Be bold, be courageous, and step into the unknown. You may not have all the details, and you may not see how it's going to work out, but along the way through the darkness, you'll see miracles. If you do this, I believe you're about to step into a new level of favor, a new level of influence, a new level of anointing. You're going to rise higher, accomplish your dreams, and reach the fullness of your destiny.

About the Author

JOEL OSTEEN is a *New York Times* bestselling author and the senior pastor of Lakewood Church in Houston, Texas. Millions connect daily with his inspirational messages through television, podcasts, Joel Osteen Radio on Sirius XM, and global digital platforms. To learn more, visit his website at JoelOsteen.com.

We Want to Hear from You!

Each week, I close our international television broadcast by giving the audience an opportunity to make Jesus the Lord of their lives. I'd like to extend that same opportunity to you. Are you at peace with God? A void exists in every person's heart that only God can fill. I'm not talking about joining a church or finding religion. I'm talking about finding life and peace and happiness. Would you pray with me today? Just say, "Lord Jesus, I repent of my sins. I ask You to come into my heart. I make You my Lord and Savior."

Friend, if you prayed that simple prayer, I believe you have been "born again." I encourage you to attend a good Bible-based church and keep God in first place in your life. For free information on how you can grow stronger in your spiritual life, please feel free to contact us.

Victoria and I love you, and we'll be praying for you. We're believing for God's best for you, that you will see your dreams come to pass. We'd love to hear from you!

To contact us, write to:

> Joel and Victoria Osteen
> PO Box #4271
> Houston, TX 77210

Or you can reach us online at joelosteen.com.